Obedience
Bible Story Puzzles

Lessons from Noah, Abraham, Moses, and Joshua

by
Enelle Eder

Carson-Dellosa Publishing Company, Inc.
Greensboro, North Carolina

It is the mission of Carson-Dellosa Christian Publishing to create
the highest-quality Scripture-based children's products that teach
the Word of God, share His love and goodness, assist in faith
development, and glorify His Son, Jesus Christ.

". . . teach me your ways so I may know you. . . ."
Exodus 33:13

To my Grandson Brayden,
May you always obey God's plan for your life.

Credits

Editor. . . . . Kathie Szitas
Inside Illustrations. . . . . Dave Schimmell
Cover Design . . . . Van Harris
Cover Illustration . . . . Marci McAdam

Scripture taken from the HOLY BIBLE, New International Reader's Version®. Copyright © 1973, 1978, 1984 by International Bible Society. Used by permission of Zondervan Publishing House. All rights reserved.

© 2008, Carson-Dellosa Publishing Company, Inc., Greensboro, North Carolina 27425. The purchase of this material entitles the buyer to reproduce activities and worksheets for home or classroom use only–not for commercial resale. Reproduction of these materials for an entire school or district is prohibited. No part of this book may be reproduced (except as noted above), stored in a retrieval system, or transmitted in any form or by any means (mechanically, electronically, recording, etc.) without the prior written consent of Carson-Dellosa Publishing Co., Inc.

Printed in the USA • All Rights Reserved.   01-023121151   ISBN: 978-1-60022-517-8

Table of Contents

Caution: Before completing any food activity, ask families' permission and inquire about students' food allergies and religious or other food preferences.

Noah, a Righteous Man

God saw that almost everyone on Earth was very sinful. God felt sorry that He had made man. There was one man who did the right things. His name was Noah. **Noah loved God and obeyed Him.**

Use the code to color the picture of Noah.

1 = blue   2 = red   3 = brown   4 = green   5 = yellow

"Noah was a godly man. He was without blame among
the people of his time. He walked with God." Genesis 6:9

4

© Carson-Dellosa

Building the Ark

God said that He was going to destroy all life on Earth with a flood. He told Noah to build an ark for himself and his family. God gave Noah all of the instructions to build the ark so that Noah and his family would be safe when the flood came. Noah did everything just as God commanded. **Noah obeyed God.**

Trace along the dashed lines to help Noah finish the ark. Then, color the picture.

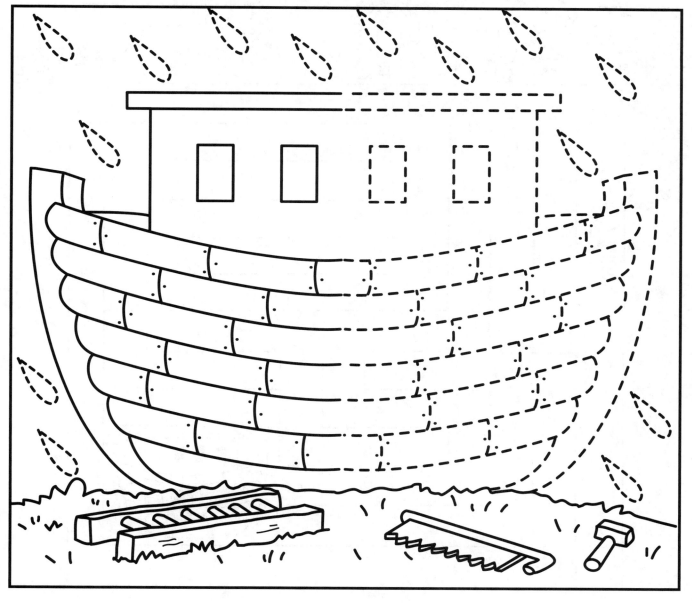

"So make yourself an ark out of cypress wood. Make
rooms in it. Cover it with tar inside and out." Genesis 6:14

The Animal Parade

God told Noah to take two of every kind of animal into the ark. God said to take one boy animal and one girl animal of every kind. All of the animals came to Noah, and he took them into the ark. **Noah listened, and he obeyed God.**

Help the animals find their way through the maze to the ark.

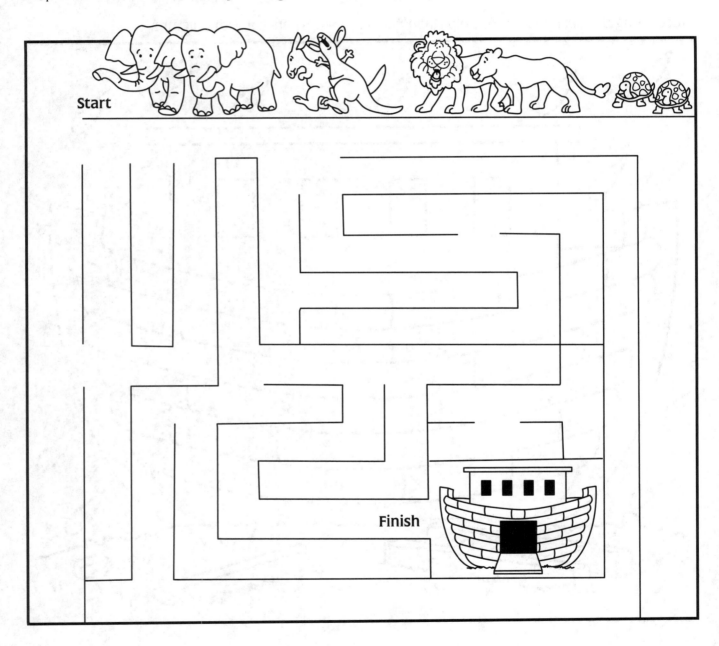

"Noah did everything the Lord commanded him to do." Genesis 7:5

© Carson-Dellosa

The Floating Zoo

Noah followed God's instructions and took all of the animals into the ark. When all the animals were safe inside, God shut the door to the ark! **Noah obeyed God.**

Find the objects hidden in the picture below.

"The animals going in were male and female of every living thing. Everything happened exactly as God had commanded Noah. Then the Lord shut him in." Genesis 7:16

God's Promise

After 40 days and 40 nights, the rain stopped. God sent a wind and the waters began to go down. After many more months, Noah and his family left the ark. Noah built an altar to thank God for keeping him and his family safe. God put a beautiful rainbow in the sky as His promise to never flood the whole earth again. God was happy because **Noah had obeyed.**

Trace the letters in the word *Promise*. Then, color the rainbow picture below using the color code.

1 = green   2 = blue   3 = purple   4 = yellow   5 = orange   6 = red

"'When the rainbow appears in the clouds, I will see it. I will remember that my covenant will last forever. It is a covenant between me and every kind of living thing on earth.'" Genesis 9:16

Noah
Whole-Group Activities

Craft

Envelope Bird Puppets

Read Genesis 8:6–12 to the children. Talk about how Noah sent a bird to see if the water had gone down. Tell the children that you are going to make bird puppets to remind them of the bird in Noah's story. Read the directions and follow the diagram.

Items Needed: 5" x 7" (12.7 cm x 17.78 cm) envelope for every two children, two wiggle eyes per child, red and black crayons, yarn, scissors, and glue

To Prepare:

1. Fold and seal the flap on the envelope.
2. Cut the envelope in half.
3. Open the cut side. Push the side of your hand into the center of the folded side and push the points together.
4. Put your hand inside (four fingers in the upper side and thumb in the bottom) and bring the points together. Shape the points for a beak.
5. Glue on wiggle eyes. Draw two black nostrils on the tip of the beak. Draw a red tongue inside the beak.
6. Cut yarn into 1" (2.54 cm) inch pieces. Glue yarn above the eyes along the top of the face.
7. Use your bird puppet to sing this song to the tune of *Frère Jacques.*

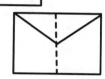

I am flying, I am flying
In the sky, in the sky.
Oh, what do I see.
It is a big tree.
Thank you, God! Thank you, God!

Noah
Whole-Group Activities

Craft

Giant Rainbow

Read Genesis 9:16 to the children. Tell the children they can make a paper rainbow. The rainbow will remind them of God's promise to never flood the whole earth again.

Items Needed: large sheet of butcher paper or bulletin board paper, 6 different colors of tissue paper (red, orange, yellow, green, blue, purple), scissors, and white glue

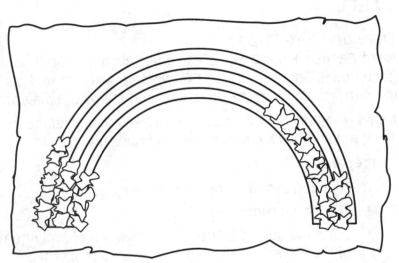

To Prepare: Draw a rainbow on the butcher paper. Cut the tissue paper into 6" (15.42 cm) squares. Smear glue on one of the stripes of the rainbow. Have each child wrap a square of tissue paper around his fist and place the rounded side on the paper–one color at a time. Continue with the rest of the stripes of the rainbow using one color per stripe. When finished, display on your classroom wall.

Snack

Hungry Hippo Haystacks

Read Genesis 6:19–22 to the children. Then, tell them you are going to make this fun snack to remind them of how Noah fed the animals on the ark.

Items Needed: 12 ounces of butterscotch chips, 2 tablespoons of peanut butter, 2 cups of chow mein noodles, and 1 cup of dry-roasted peanuts

To Prepare:
1. Put the chips and peanut butter in a microwave-safe bowl.
2. Melt for 1 minute. Stir and return to the microwave for 30 seconds. Stir again.
3. Stir in the noodles and peanuts until all are well coated.
4. Drop by spoonfuls onto wax paper, and let the snacks completely harden before serving.

Pray: *Dear Father, thank You for providing for and protecting Noah and the animals. Thank You for providing for us each day. You are always faithful to Your promises. Help us to honor the promises we make to others in our lives. Amen.*

Moving Day

One day the Lord came to a man named Abram. (God later changed Abram's name to Abraham.) God told Abram to move to a new land that he would show him. God said that he would bless Abram there, and make him the father of a great nation. **Abraham obeyed God.**

Help Abraham and his wife Sarah find the new land.

"So Abram left, just as the Lord had told him." Genesis 12:4

Abraham Becomes Rich

The Lord blessed Abraham. He made him rich in cattle, sheep, and servants. Abraham's nephew Lot traveled with him. He also had flocks of sheep and herds of cattle. **Abraham obeyed God, and God blessed Abraham.**

Find and circle the sheep that is not the same as the others.

"Abram had become very rich. He had a lot of livestock and silver and gold.
Lot was moving around with Abram. Lot also had flocks and herds and tents." Genesis 13:2,5

12 © Carson-Dellosa

Abraham Builds an Altar

The land became too crowded for both Abraham and Lot's flocks and herds. Abraham wanted to keep peace among everyone, so he let Lot choose first which part of the land he wanted. Then, God told Abraham that the rest of the land would be his. Abraham moved to this land and built an altar to worship and thank God. **God was pleased with Abraham's obedience.**

To see the altar Abraham built, color the shapes that have an **A** on them brown. Color the shapes with a **B** on them green. Then, color the rest of the picture.

"'Go. Walk through the land. . . . I am giving it to you.'
So Abram moved his tents. He went to live near the large trees of
Mamre at Hebron. There he built an altar to honor the Lord." Genesis 13:17–18

A Starry Promise

Abraham was growing older, and he and Sarah still didn't have any children. But God was pleased with Abraham's obedience and told him that he would have many children. **Abraham trusted and obeyed God.**

Follow the lines from the stars and write each letter in its correct space to see what God said to Abraham.

"'Look up at the sky. Count the stars, if you can.' Then he said to him, 'That is how many children you will have.'" Genesis 15:5

14

© Carson-Dellosa

Abraham's Son

When Abraham was 99 years old, God came to visit him. God said, "Sarah will have a son." Sarah laughed because she was 90 years old. But God's promise was true. A year later, she had a son named Isaac, which means *laughter*. **God blessed Abraham and Sarah because they obeyed Him.**

Connect the dots 1–20.

"Abraham was 100 years old when his son Isaac was born to him." Genesis 21:5

Abraham
Whole-Group Activities

Craft

Star Puppets

Items Needed: star patterns (page 17), construction paper, crayons or markers, glue, one craft stick for each child, clear tape, two wiggle eyes per child, two cotton balls per child, brown or black yarn, one 4" x 8" (10.6 cm x 15.24 cm) piece of flannel or cloth per child

To Prepare:

1. Cut two large stars and one small star from construction paper using the star patterns (page 17) as templates. The two large stars will be for Abraham and Sarah. The smaller star will be used to make an Isaac puppet.
2. Color the center of each star, leaving the bottom, top, and side point tips uncolored for the feet, face, and hands.
3. Draw a mouth and nose on each top portion of the star.
4. Glue on two wiggle eyes (or cut two circles from paper).
5. Glue on cotton for hair, beard, and moustache for Abraham. Glue on pieces of yarn to create hair for Sarah and Isaac. Wrap a piece of flannel or other cloth around Isaac and tape in place.
6. Fold the two side points in for arms. Tape a craft stick on the back.

Skit

Star Puppet Skit

Use the star puppets of Abraham, Sarah, and Isaac to present this skit.

Sarah: Oh, Abraham, I am so tired. Do we really have to move again?

Abraham: Yes, my dear wife. We must obey God. He said that He will bless us with many children and grandchildren.

Sarah: I know we must obey. Yet, I want to have a child now.

Abraham: I do too, but we must wait for God's time.

Sarah: All right, I will go, but this time I'm not going to move your dried cactus collection! *(Puppets leave, then come back as Sarah laughs.)*

Abraham: Sarah, why are you laughing?

Sarah: You remember what the visitor said? He said I will have a son next year. I am 90 years old and too old to have a child!

Abraham: God promised it. I have obeyed Him all my life, and I believe God's promises. *(Both puppets leave as Sarah continues to laugh. Say or hold up a sign that reads "One year later." Then, Abraham and Sarah, holding Isaac, come back.)*

Sarah: Oh look, Abraham! He is so precious! I think he has your eyes!

Abraham: God has kept His promise to us, Sarah. He has given us a son. It pays to obey God.

    © Carson-Dellosa

Star Patterns

Baby Moses in a Basket

When Moses was a baby, a wicked king demanded that all the Hebrew boy babies be killed. Moses' mother was not afraid to disobey the king's order. She put Moses in a basket and placed the basket in the Nile River. **Moses' mother trusted God.**

Connect the numbers 1–15 to see what kept Moses afloat in the Nile River.

"So she got a basket that was made out of the stems of tall grass. . . . Then she placed the child in it. She put the basket in the tall grass that grew along the bank of the Nile River." Exodus 2:3

18 © Carson-Dellosa

God's Plan for Moses

A princess, the daughter of a great pharaoh, was by the river when she saw the basket carrying Moses. She felt sorry for the baby and took him back to the palace to live as her son. By showing compassion, **the princess was obeying God's plan.**

Find and circle the objects hidden in the picture.

"When she opened [the basket], she saw the baby. He was crying. She felt sorry for him." Exodus 2:6

© Carson-Dellosa

19

The Burning Bush

Moses grew up, left Egypt, and went to the land of Midian. While he was there, God spoke to him from a burning bush. God told Moses to go back to Egypt to free the Hebrew people from slavery. Moses didn't think that the pharaoh or anyone would listen to him, but **he obeyed God.**

Use the code to color Moses and the burning bush.

1 = gray   2 = yellow   3 = orange   4 = blue   5 = brown   6 = green

"There the angel of the Lord appeared to him from inside a burning bush.
Moses saw that the bush was on fire. But it didn't burn up." Exodus 3:2

A Stubborn Pharaoh

Moses and his brother Aaron went to the pharaoh and told him that God said to let the Hebrew people leave Egypt. The pharaoh wanted to keep using the Hebrews for slaves, so he said "No!" The pharaoh's heart was stubborn and hard. He did not obey God. However, Moses did not stop doing what God asked. **Moses obeyed God.**

When we do what God wants us to do, we are obeying God and our hearts are soft toward God. Color the pictures that show how we can obey God.

"In spite of that, Pharaoh's heart became stubborn. He wouldn't listen to them, just as the Lord had said." Exodus 7:13

The Plagues

God was not happy with the stubborn pharaoh. He sent nine plagues: water changing into blood, frogs, gnats, flies, a plague on livestock, boils, hail, locusts, and darkness. Still, the pharaoh would not let the Hebrew people go. The tenth plague took the lives of the firstborn sons of all Egyptian families. The Hebrew families' firstborn sons were spared because they put lambs blood on their doorframes. Finally, the pharaoh said, "Take the Hebrews and go!" **At last, the pharaoh obeyed God.**

Match the letters with the pictures. Then, write the letters on the lines below to find out what God wanted the pharaoh to do.

"During the night, Pharaoh sent for Moses and Aaron. He said to them, 'Get out of here! You and the Israelites, leave my people! Go. Worship the Lord, just as you have asked.'" Exodus 12:31

Moses
Whole-Group Activities

Craft

The Red Sea

Read Exodus 14:21–22. Tell the children that after the pharaoh let the Hebrew people go, he changed his mind. The pharaoh and his men chased after them. When Moses and the people got to the Red Sea, they had no way to escape. God told Moses to stretch out his hand. Moses obeyed, and the water of the Red Sea rolled back, allowing Moses and the people to escape on dry land. When the pharaoh's army arrived and tried to follow them, the water rolled back around them. Tell the children they will make a Red Sea to remind them that God is faithful to those who obey Him.

Items Needed: one 6" x 9" (15.24 cm x 22.86 cm) or smaller piece of cardboard (back of a memo pad, for example) for each child, brown bags, blue construction paper, three chenille craft sticks for each child, scissors, glue, crayons or markers

To Prepare: The Red Sea

1. Cut a section from a brown paper bag to fit the cardboard. Glue the paper onto one side of the cardboard. Decorate the brown paper with fish, rocks and other items found at the bottom of the sea.

2. Cut a 6" X 11 1/2" (15.24 cm x 29.21 cm) piece of blue construction paper. Cut the construction paper in half.

3. Cut a wave pattern along one of the 6" (15.24 cm) edges of each piece of construction paper.

4. Create a 1/4"(0.635 cm) tab along the 6" (15.24 cm) straight edge of the construction paper. Glue the tab to the 6" (15.24 cm) edge of the bottom (nonpaper side) of the cardboard. Fold the both panels of construction paper over the brown paper side of the cardboard. The construction paper should overlap.

To Prepare: People

Allow the children to make more than one of these fun chenille-craft-stick people to use to act out the story of the crossing of the Red Sea. For Moses, use scraps of cloth and a brown chenille craft stick for a staff.

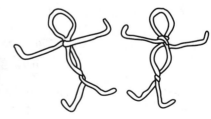

1. Begin with one whole and one half chenille craft sticks. Fold the whole one in half. Create a loop for the head and twist together to secure in place.

2. Twist the two ends together to create the body and legs. Bend up the ends to create feet.

3. Wrap the half chenille craft stick around the head to create the arms.

Moses
Whole-Group Activities

Game

The Ten Commandments Game

Read to the children the Ten Commandments from Exodus 20:1–17, or read the paraphrased version listed inside the scroll.

Items Needed: brown paper bag or other piece of large paper, twine

To Prepare:

1. Cut out one side of a brown paper bag and lay flat.
2. Write the Ten Commandments on the paper.
3. Roll up like a scroll and wrap the piece of twine around the scroll to hold it closed.

Tell the children that God gave Moses 10 special rules for the Israelites to follow and that we are to follow them, too. Tell the children that God gave these special rules, called commandments, to Moses on special stone tablets. Today, however, you will read them from a special scroll. Open the scroll and read the commandments to the children. When you are finished, roll up the paper and secure with the twine to prepare to play the game.

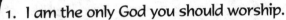

1. I am the only God you should worship.
2. Never make or worship any idols.
3. Never use my name for swearing.
4. Set aside Sundays to rest and worship.
5. Obey your father and mother.
6. Never kill anyone.
7. Husbands and wives must be faithful to each other.
8. Never steal.
9. Never tell a lie.
10. Never be jealous of what someone else has.

Game Rules

Put children in a circle. Designate one child as "it" or "the rule carrier." Give her the rolled-up paper. Have her skip around the children in the circle as they sing this song to the tune of "The Mulberry Bush."

God gave us 10 special rules, 10 special rules, 10 special rules.
God gave us 10 special rules, to follow every day.

When the song stops, the child stops and drops the roll of paper behind the child she is behind. That child then picks up the paper and chases the first child around the circle. The first child tries to get back to the empty space before she is caught. If she is successful, the child with the roll is "it." The game continues until everyone has had a turn at being "the rule carrier."

A Land of Milk and Honey

God kept His promise and led His people to the promised land. When they were near, Moses sent out spies, including a man named Joshua, to explore the land. Joshua came back and said it was a land full of good food like milk and honey and fruit–just like God had promised. Joshua said there were giants living there too, but with God's help they could take the land! **Joshua obeyed Moses and God.**

Find and circle the words from the word bank in the word-search puzzle.

Word Bank

MILK   HONEY

SPIES   LAND

A S D F H
J P G P O
M I L K N
I E H N E
O S L M Y
K L A N D

"If the Lord is pleased with us, he'll lead us into that land. It's a land that has plenty of milk and honey. He'll give it to us." Numbers 14:8

Moses Chooses Joshua

When Moses was very old, God told him to appoint a new leader for the Israelites. The new leader had to be brave, strong, and obedient to God. Moses chose a new leader that was brave, strong, and obedient to God. God was pleased with Moses' choice. **God knew the new leader would obey Him.**

Match the picture with the vowels. Then, write the letters on the lines to find the name of the new leader.

"Then I sent for Joshua. I spoke to him in front of all of the people of Israel. I said, 'Be strong and brave. You must go with these people. They are going into the land the Lord promised with an oath to give to their fathers.'" Deuteronomy 31:7

Rahab and the Spies

Joshua told the Israelites that the Lord said it was time to conquer the land He had promised to them. Joshua sent two spies into the city of Jericho. Soldiers inside Jericho saw the spies and began to chase them. A woman named Rahab brought them into her home and hid them on the roof. The only thing Rahab asked in return was that they keep her family safe when their army came back to conquer the city. **Rahab obeyed God's plan.**

Find the two spies that are hiding and circle them.

"'Now then, please take an oath. Promise me in the name
of the Lord that you will be kind to my family. I've been kind to you.'" Joshua 2:12

Name _____

Crossing the Jordan

The Israelites were ready to conquer Jericho. Joshua led them to the edge of the Jordan River. The water was overflowing its banks, and they could not cross. God told Joshua to tell the priests who were carrying the Ark of the Covenant to step into the edge of the water. When they did, the waters rolled back, just as they had done at the Red Sea for Moses and their grandparents! **Joshua obeyed God. God took care of the Israelites because they obeyed Him.**

Color in RED the shapes with a ✝⃝ on them. Color in BLUE the shapes with a ✝ on them.

"The priests carried the ark of the covenant of the Lord. They stood firm on dry ground in the middle of the river." Joshua 3:17

© Carson-Dellosa

The Battle of Jericho

God told Joshua to silently march with his men around the wall of Jericho for six days. Then, on the seventh day, the priests were to blow trumpets and shout loudly. When they did this, the wall around Jericho fell. Joshua and his army conquered the city because **Joshua obeyed God.**

Help Joshua find his way to Jericho.

"The priests blew the trumpets. As soon as the fighting men heard the sound, they gave a loud shout. Then the wall fell down. Every man charged straight in. So they took the city." Joshua 6:20

29

Joshua
Whole-Group Activities

Jericho Walls

Tell the children that you are going to make a wall so that you can retell the story of the wall of Jericho falling down.

Items Needed: 24 large, brown grocery bags, lots of old newspaper and masking tape

To Prepare:

1. Have the children stuff 12 brown bags with crumpled newspaper.
2. Open the other bags and pull them over top of the newspaper-filled bags.
3. Tape the edges with masking tape.
4. Repeat until you have 12 large blocks.

Build the wall 4 blocks long and 3 blocks high.
Have the children march quietly around the wall six times. On the seventh time, instruct the children to shout, "GOD IS GREAT!" Designate a child to bump the wall so that it will fall over.

Craft

Medallions

Read Joshua 24:24 to the children. Tell the children that when Joshua was getting old, he called the Israelites together. He reminded them of things the Lord had done for them and encouraged them to serve God. Have the children name things that the Lord has done for them and then help them to make medallions to remind them to always love, serve, and obey God. Children can wear the medallions around their necks or hang them in their rooms.

Items Needed: card stock, copies of the medallion patterns (page 31) for each child, glue sticks, scissors, glitter, paper punch, crayons or markers, and yarn

To Prepare:

1. Have the children decorate and cut out each medallion pattern.
2. Punch a hole near the top edge.
3. Smear the glue stick around the edge of the circle on the front and sprinkle with glitter.
4. Thread a piece of yarn through the hole and tie in a knot.

 © Carson-Dellosa

Medallion Patterns

Noah, Abraham, Moses, and Joshua
Review

God made it very clear to the people of the Old Testament that they should obey Him. Things went much better for them when they did. **God tells us in His Word that we should obey Him, too.**

Draw a line to match each Old Testament man with an item that was in his story.

"I also gave them another command. I said, 'Obey me.
Then I will be your God. And you will be my people.'" Jeremiah 7:23

© Carson-Dellosa